EDITED, WITH COMMENTARY BY PIERCE G. FREDERICKS   DESIGNED BY ANTHONY LAROTUN

THE CIVIL WAR

ABRAHAM LINCOLN'S IMMORTAL WORDS

ALLERY EDITION • BANTAM BOOKS • NEW YORK

AS THEY KNEW IT

AND MATHEW BRADY'S FAMOUS PHOTOGRAPHS

In this book, Pierce G. Fredericks of The New York Times has combined two uniquely distinctive statements about the Civil War: the words of the President of the United States and the pictures of the first photographer to cover an entire war. Working from the massive collection of Lincoln's papers and the enormous treasury of Brady's photographs housed in the Library of Congress and National Archives, Mr. Fredericks reveals the most memorable conflict in American history as these two eyewitnesses knew it.

TO BEGIN WITH...

Why was there an American Civil War? The men who fought it would have said that the question was whether a state or states had the right to secede from the Union. Later historians would talk of the economic conflicts between the agricultural South and the industrial North. In the end, though, the answer has to be "slavery." The other problems were certainly there, but the big one that boiled over into war was slavery.

As the Nineteenth Century rounded into its second half, America was moving west. The South was determined that slavery should move west too and the North was just as determined that it should not. Pro- and anti-slavery men flooded into the new territory of Kansas, readying for the day when it would vote to become a free or a slave state. Southerners raided the abolitionist stronghold at Lawrence, Kansas, and left two men dead. A hard-eyed Yankee, John Brown by name, struck back by killing five Southerners. In 1859, the same Brown would seize the Federal Arsenal at Harpers Ferry, Virginia, with plans for raising a slave rebellion. Marines, under a Regular Army colonel named Robert E. Lee, would march in and take Brown for hanging.

In 1860, Abraham Lincoln, who had already noted that ". . . this Government cannot endure permanently half slave and half free," won the Presidency over the candidates of a divided Democratic Party. Even before he was inaugurated, he said flatly that no slavery would be allowed to go west to the new states. In February, 1861, the frustrated South inaugurated Jefferson Davis as president of the seven states which had then seceded and the nation was on the road to a war which would last four years.

This book is the story of that war in Lincoln's words and in photographs by the great photographer Mathew Brady and others. Lincoln had posed for Brady in February, 1860, when he came to New York to speak at Cooper Union; of the resulting portrait (right) Lincoln later said, "Brady and the Cooper Union Institute made me President."

18

Amid rumors of plots to assassinate him, Lincoln was smuggled into Washington on a closed train. There, quavery President James Buchanan was treating with delegates from the new Confederacy who were demanding that Union troops get out of the South and surrender Fort Sumter in Charleston, South Carolina harbor. Inauguration Day was March 4, 1861. Lincoln rode to the Capitol, its new dome still half finished (right), to make a last appeal. "I hold," he said, "that in contemplation of universal law, and of the Constitution, the Union of these States is perpetual. . . . It is safe to assert that no government proper ever had a provision in its organic law for its own termination . . . no state upon its own mere motion, can lawfully get out of the Union." Then he made his own course unmistakably clear:

In your hands, my dissatisfied fellow countrymen, and not in mine, is the momentous issue of civil war. The government will not assail you. You can have no conflict, without being yourselves the aggressors. You have no oath registered in Heaven to destroy the government, while I have the most solemn one to ''preserve, protect and defend'' it.

Jefferson Davis (left) was the
President of the Confederacy and he'd
never expected the job. A
Kentuckian and a West Pointer, he'd
left the army to become a Mississippi
planter famous for his kindness
to his slaves. He had
expected a military role if war came,
but now he was a chief of state—
and it was work in which he had very
little experience. Lincoln, with
his usual perception, had seen him
as the most likely head of the
deep South, slave-holding states:

They tell us that they desire the people
of a territory to vote slavery out
or in as they please ... It is the surest
way of nationalizing the institution.
Just as certain, but more dangerous
because more insidious; but it is leading
us there just as certainly and as surely
as Jeff. Davis himself would have us go.

Lincoln's problem was two-fold: to
take action against the states
which had seceded, but to put the re-
sponsibility for any act leading
to war on the South. His decision was
to send another supply ship to
Sumter where Union Major Robert
Anderson (above) faced Confederate
batteries commanded by General
P.G.T. Beauregard (right). A
message went to the Navy Department:

Steamers Pocahontas at Norfolk, Pawnee at
Washington, and Revenue Cutter Harriet
Lane at N. York to be ready under sailing
orders for sea with one months stores.
Three hundred seamen to be kept ready
for leaving the receiving ship at N. York.

*Major Anderson held Sumter (below)
with two companies of U.S. Regulars and
supplies to keep him going until
the middle of April. When Beauregard
opened fire at 4:30 A.M. on April
12, 1861, Anderson had, at best, only
a few days before his food would
have run out. The first shot was
good, bursting squarely over the
fort, and the Confederate gunners followed with surprisingly ac-
curate fire which burned the wooden
barracks inside Sumter. The ship
Lincoln sent did not get through and
the fire in the fort was threatening to blow the powder magazines.
On the afternoon of April 13,
Anderson, whose orders did not say
that he was to hold out at all*

costs, surrendered. There was now
a war on and Lincoln made it official:

A PROCLAMATION

Whereas the Laws of the United States have
been for some time past, and now are
opposed, and the execution thereof ob-
structed, in the States of South Carolina,
Georgia, Alabama, Florida, Mississippi,
Louisiana and Texas, by combinations too
powerful to be suppressed by the ord-
inary course of judicial proceedings, or
by the powers vested in the Marshals by law,

Now, therefore, I, Abraham Lincoln, President of the United States, in virtue
of the power in me vested by the Constitution and the laws have thought fit
to call forth, and hereby do call
forth the militia of the several States
of the Union, to the aggregate number
of seventy-five thousand, in order
to suppress said combinations and
to cause the laws to be duly executed.

*To fight this war, Lincoln had an
army of 17,000 regulars, scattered
through the Indian country, and
an antique commander, General Winfield
Scott (right, seated), the aging
hero of the Mexican War. Scott had
a good head on him, though, and
he warned his President that this
would be a long struggle. Lincoln
listened—as he had listened
to Scott before he became President:*

**Mr. Lincoln tenders his sincere thanks to
Gen. Scott, for the copy of 'his views
Etc.' which is received; and especially
for this renewed manifestation of
his patriotic purposes as a citizen, con-
nected, as it is, with his high
official position, and most distinguished character, as a military captain.**

With the calls for troops, four more
states—Virginia, Tennessee, North
Carolina and Arkansas—swung
over to join the original seven
of the Confederacy. That made eleven
Southern states against twenty-
three Northern. The North's advantage in manpower was something like
two to one overall, something like
four to one if slaves were   .
excepted and only whites counted.
Signs pointed to an easy victory
over the Confederates (right), but
even so early in the struggle
Lincoln saw the need to make it more
than a military conquest. He
told a special session of Congress:

This is essentially a People's contest.
On the side of the Union it is a struggle
for maintaining in the world, that form
and substance of government whose leading
object is, to elevate the condition
of men . . . to lift artificial weights
from all shoulders—to clear the
paths of laudable pursuit for all—to
afford all, an unfettered state,
and a fair chance, in the face of life.

*As the Union men (left) came in
the regiments arrived in Washington
and it was common for them to march
past the White House and call
for their Commander-in-Chief. He ap-
peared before one such group and said:*

Gentlemen, I appear before you in
obedience to your call; not however, to
make a speech. I have made a great many
poor speeches in my life, and feel
considerably relieved now to know that
the dignity of the position in which
I have been placed does not permit me to
expose myself any longer (laughter) ... I
thank you for the kindness of your
call, but I must keep good my word and
not be led into a speech as I told
you I did not appear for that purpose.

There was more to the war than the
land, though, and, curiously, it was
Winfield Scott—a soldier—who saw
how it was to be won at sea.
The South was poor in every kind
of manufacturing. Secessionist states
had taken some arms from local
Federal Arsenals, but in the long
run the Confederacy must import her
arms or die. There was neither a
Southern navy nor the means to
build one. Put a blockade around

*the South, said the old General,
keep foreign merchant ships from
reaching her and she will go under.
They called it "Scott's Anaconda"—
a strangling python. Lincoln listened,
called for sailors (above) and
proclaimed a blockade of the coast.*

Now, therefore, I, Abraham Lincoln, President of the United States . . . have further deemed it advisable to set on foot a blockade of the States aforesaid.

29

. . . if any person, under the pretended authority of the said States, or under any other pretense shall molest a vessel of the United States, or the persons or cargo on board of her, such person will be held amenable to the laws of the United States for the prevention and punishment of piracy.

To make that blockade good, almost anything that would float was purchased and a few guns put aboard her (right). Even old ferry boats were armed to work the shallow rivers that ran to the coast.

*Lincoln's soldiers came to Washington
—led by bands, often decked out in
fancy uniforms and bearing flags carefully stitched by their hometown
womenfolk. The President often found
himself embroiled in even the small-
est details of the new army:*

**To Whom It May Concern: The bearer of this,
Hugh Roden, says he is a drummer in
the seventh regiment New Jersey volunteers, and wishes to be transferred to the
second regiment New Jersey volunteers,
to be with his brother, who is in the lat-
ter regiment. If it will not
injuriously affect the service, I
shall be glad for him to be obliged.**

---

*Then it was time to fight—or rather
Lincoln was anxious for action before the militia's three month term
of service expired. Under General
Irvin McDowell, 30,000 men—civilians
trailing along as on a picnic
—marched out to face Beauregard's
22,000 Confederates at Manassas
Junction. In they went against Beauregard's left flank and threatened to
roll it up until Thomas Jackson
won his nickname by standing like a
stone wall. Then more Confederates
came up to take the Yankees in
the rear and the victory became
a defeat and then it became a rout.*

*Back over Bull Run's little bridge
(left) they fled, their dead still on
the field and there were more
letters for Lincoln to write to be-
reaved parents. This one had gone
to Ephraim Ellsworth and his wife
Phoebe when their son Elmer had
been killed a little earlier in a
skirmish at Alexandria, Virginia.*

In the untimely loss of your noble son,
our affliction here, is scarcely less than
your own. So much of promised
usefulness to one's country, and of
bright hopes for one's self and friends,
have been suddenly dashed, as in his fall.

In the hope that it may be no intrusion
upon the sacredness of your sorrow,
I have ventured to address you this tri-
bute to the memory of my young friend,
and your brave and early fallen child.

May God give you that consolation which is beyond all earthly power.

Out west, the opening struggle cen-
tered in St. Louis, Missouri.
The Union men rallied on
tough politico Francis P. Blair
and his rough right arm, General
Nathaniel Lyon. Lyon only had some
6,000 men. The Confederates
had almost twice that many.
The red-bearded Lyon led
his 6,000 into battle at Wilson's
Creek in August. Before the fight
was finished, Lyon was dead.
The Confederates had won the day,
but for the moment showed no
inclination to advance further. At
least the northern half of Missouri
was safe for the Union and in west-
ern Virginia, General George
McClellan won two small fights which
helped the state-to-be of West
Virginia stay in the anti-slavery
camp. Lincoln took pen in hand:

Will Lieut. Gen. Scott please consider and
inform me what can be, and
ought to be done as a recognition
of the gallantry of the officers who
fought with Gen. Lyon at Wilson's Creek?

*Clearly, a three month militia was not
going to be enough to win this war.
Congress passed a bill calling for
half a million volunteers to serve for
three years and, stung by the early
set-backs, the North hurried to provide the quota. Clearly, too, these
men were going to need proper
training. General George McClellan
(right), whose two small victories in
West Virginia were the Union's
greatest success story to date,
was brought east for the job. He
was a West Point man who had retired
a few years before the war to
go into the railroad business. When
Scott retired, Lincoln wrote him:*

**Lt. Genl. Scott having been, upon his own
application placed on the list of
retired officers, with his advice, and
the concurrence of the entire cabinet,
I have designated you to command
the whole Army. You will, therefore, as-
sume this enlarged duty at once,
conferring with me so far as necessary.**

---

*McClellan rarely felt any need to
confer with Lincoln, but he did turn
out to be a splendid drill master.*

18

*While McClellan drilled, another West
Pointer, retired but returned to
service for the war, found himself
with a small command at Cairo,
Illinois. Nobody thought much of the
man. His name was Ulysses S. Grant
(right) and there were many people who
said he was a drunk. A restless
soul without any very precise orders,
he took his men and a few jerry-
built gunboats up the Tennessee
River and captured Confederate Fort
Henry. Then, cutting telegraph
lines so no one could tell him to
stop, he turned to much more heavily
defended Fort Donelson. His gunboats were knocked around, but Grant
kept right on attacking until the
Confederates asked for terms. He
sent back "No terms except an uncon-
ditional surrender can be accepted.
I propose to move immediately
upon your works." Donelson surrendered. Some Prohibitionists came
to see Lincoln to complain about
Grant's drinking and he told them:*

**What brand does he drink? I'd like to
send a barrel of it to the other generals.**

The Union blockade was making itself felt. Luxuries were already very short in the South and far more important items would soon be too, were no way found to drive the Union Navy off the Southern ports. At Norfolk, Virginia, a young Confederate officer thought he knew how to do it and set about building a ship whose sides would be armoured with iron. In the North, though, another armoured ship was building, a tiny thing; a "pill box on a raft" was the name someone would hang on her. She was the design of an inventive Swede, John Ericsson (right); her name was the Monitor *and shortly she would meet the Confederate* Merrimack *in the first battle of ironclads—a battle which would make every other ship in every other Navy in the world obsolete. At first, Lincoln was not impressed with the new design. He wrote his Secretary of the Navy:*

I have just seen Lieut. Worden who says the Monitor could be boarded and captured very easily—first, after boarding, by wedging the turret, so that it would not turn, and then by pouring water in her & drowning her machinery. He is decidedly of the opinion she should not go sky-larking up to Norfolk.

The Confederate Merrimack *steamed into Hampton Roads and blasted the helpless wooden Union frigates. Then, with Washington in a panic, little* Monitor *(left) steamed up—almost sinking on the way—and hammered* Merrimack *back into Norfolk, never to sortie again. The President wrote:*

I most cordially recommend that Commander
John L. Worden, U.S. Navy, receive a
vote of thanks of Congress for the eminent
skill and gallantry, exhibited by
him in the late remarkable battle between
the U.S. Iron clad steamer Monitor,
under his command, and the Rebel
Iron clad Steamer Merrimack, in March last.

*McClellan still drilled and dreamed
of sailing his troops down the
Chesapeake, then attacking overland
toward Richmond. To Lincoln, the
move seemed to leave Washington
exposed; he wrote to his general:*

You and I have distinct and different
plans for a movement of the Army of the
Potomac—yours to be down the
Chesapeake, up the Rappahannock to
Urbana, and across land to the terminus
of the Railroad on the York River—mine
to move directly to a point
on the Railroad South West of Manassas.

*In the end, McClellan had his way
and sailed off, complaining about the
40,000 men he had left to defend
Washington. In Yorktown, however, instead of attacking the paper-thin
Confederate defences, he set up elab-
orate siege operations (right).
It was all too slow to suit Lincoln:*

You now have over one hundred thousand
troops . . . I think you better break
the enemies' line from Yorktown to Warwick
River at once. They will probably
use time, as advantageously as you can.

McClellan stood in front of Yorktown for a month, then moved up the Peninsula, building roads (left) as he went. At Seven Pines, only five miles from Richmond, he stopped to tidy up again. While he tidied, the out-numbered Confederates of Joe Johnston attacked during a drenching rain storm. Back reeled McClellan and though he counter-attacked to regain the position, the drill master began to have severe doubts about whether he really had enough men to get on to Richmond after all. His task was not made lighter by Lincoln who was worried about a threat to Washington from Confederates in the Shenandoah Valley.

I think the time is near when you must either attack Richmond or give up the job and come to the defence of Washington. Let me hear from you instantly.

To make McClellan yet unhappier, he had with him the detective Allan Pinkerton (left). Pinkerton, founder of one of the first detective agencies in America, had known McClellan in the railroad business and followed him east when he became commander of the army. A good detective, he was something less than the ideal military intelligence operative. He had, in fact, almost a genius for seeing two Confederates where but one existed and McClellan, already groggy from Johnston's blow, was only too willing to believe his agent's report that some 200,000 of the enemy stood between him and his goal.

*By far the worst misfortune to befall
McClellan was a wound Joe Johnston
received at the Battle of Seven Pines.
To replace him, the Confederacy
chose Robert E. Lee (right). He was
considered the finest officer in
the pre-war army; indeed, he had
been offered command of the Union
forces, but had decided to go with
his home state of Virginia.
He took over with a crisis before
him. Lincoln had wired McClellan:*

**Stripped bare, as we are here, it
will be all we can do to prevent them
from crossing the Potomac ... Please
understand this and do the best you can
with the force you have.**

---

*Now Lincoln relented and was about to
send another 40,000 men. Lee had
to create a diversion to hold the
men near Washington. Promptly, he
sent one more division to Stonewall
Jackson in the Shenandoah Valley and
told him to raise the devil there.*

The stern Jackson (right) did not have to be told twice. Using his out-numbered men as "foot cavalry," he raced them through the Valley so quickly that the three Union forces sent against him were smashed individually before they were able to assemble. He simply out-ran them while Lincoln urged his own field commanders to show a little of the same speed—which they did not.

I think the evidence now preponderates that Ewell and Jackson are still about Winchester. Assuming this, it is, for you, a question of legs. Put in all the speed you can.

Lee had weakened himself to support the Valley, but McClellan sat on the marshy Peninsula (below), complained and received a wire from Washington:

Your three dispatches . . . suggesting
the probability of your being overwhelm-
ed by 200,000, and talking of where
the responsibility will belong
pains me very much. I give you all I can.

Jackson raced down from the Valley to join Lee. Quickly, Lee struck, trying to cut McClellan off from his line of supply. The victory was incomplete, but it alarmed Lincoln:

Save the Army—first, where you are, if you can, and secondly by removal if you must. P.S. If, at any time, you feel able to take the offensive, you are not restrained from doing so.

Lee struck again, but it served only
to push McClellan up against the
James River where he could be supported by supply ships. On a
crest along the river, the Union
artillery (above) took position, the
guns almost hub to hub. The Confederates went in with a rebel yell,
but the Union batteries blew them
away almost before they were started.
The Peninsula campaign was over.

If the news for the Confederacy was good at Richmond, it was bad elsewhere. The Union Navy had taken a semi-retired admiral named David Glasgow Farragut (left) out of mothballs and sent him against New Orleans. The greatest port of the Confederacy was defended by a fleet and by forts along its channel. Farragut shot the fleet to bits and his mortar boats (over page) beat down the forts. The blockade that was throttling the Confederacy was that much tighter. More and more the hope of the South lay in some brilliant success which would encourage intervention from Europe.

A jubilant Lincoln wrote to Congress

I submit, herewith, a list of naval officers who commanded vessels in the recent brilliant operations of the squadron commanded by Flag-Officer

Farragut, which led to the capture of
Forts Jackson and St. Phillip, city
of New Orleans and the destruction of
rebel gunboats, rams etc. in April, 1862.
For their services and gallantry on
those occasions I cordially recommend
that they should, by name, receive
a vote of thanks from the Congress.

*And out west, Confederate Albert
Sidney Johnston (right) led 40,000
men against Grant who had come up
the Tennessee River to Shiloh. Grant
was having a bad day—his forces
were dispersed and his pickets were
nodding. Johnston gained a complete
surprise in an April Sunday dawn attack,
and the Northerners were sent reeling
back to the river bank. Grant just
managed to hold on; Johnston fell
mortally wounded and night came. The
next morning, Grant's reserve came
up. Two gunboats pounded the Confederate flank and drove them
from the field. The losses were
10,000 men on each side. Lincoln
began to take notice of this Grant:*

I congratulate you and all concerned on your
recent victories. How does it all sum up?

Slowly, a Union army was coming into being. Its officers were learning their business and were getting troops—battle toughened men and boys (right) of whom the South could no longer say that one Confederate was worth two—or four— or however many you like—Yankees.

To forestall a second Valley cam-
paign Lincoln called General John
Pope (right) from the west. Pope fought
at Manassas and Lee ran circles
around the bewildered newcomer.
Lincoln sent out frustrated telegrams:

Do you hear any thing from Pope?

What news from the front?

Any news from Gen. Pope?

What news?

Please send me the latest news.

Before long, Pope was back in Wash-
ington, glad to have saved his skin,
and Lee was preparing to move north
for the big win the South so badly
needed to get foreign recognition.

Lee planned to move north behind the Shenandoah ridges, heading for Hagerstown, Maryland, then turning through one of the mountain passes to fall on the unsuspecting Union army as it came out from Washington to give pursuit. On the way up, he detailed Stonewall Jackson to capture the Northern garrison at Harpers' Ferry (right), and then rejoin. Lincoln tried to get news from frightened Governor Curtin of Pennsylvania:

Please tell me at once, what is your latest news from, or towards, Hagerstown or of the enemies movements in any direction.

*McClellan came racing up from
the Peninsula and Lincoln wired:*

Your despatches of today received. God
bless you, and all with you.
Destroy the rebel army, if possible.

And to worried Governor Curtin went:

Since telegraphing you, despatch from
Gen. McClellan, dated 7 o'clock this morning. Nothing of importance happened to

him yesterday. This morning he was
up with the enemy at Sharpsburg, and
waiting for a heavy fog to rise.

---

*And before McClellan lay an oppor-
tunity which rarely comes to any general. A copy of Lee's order detach-
ing Jackson had been captured by
Union cavalry. McClellan knew his foe
was divided. He could destroy the halves
separately if he got into action (above)
as fast as Stonewall Jackson would have.*

*McClellan dawdled north for a whole
day. Lee, finding the Yankees close
behind, set his men at Sharpsburg,
behind Antietam Creek and sent
word for Jackson to come running.
McClellan dawdled another day, Jackson came up and when McClellan
finally attacked on the morning of
September 17, he hit the northern end
of Lee's line only. Through the
morning they battled with dreadful
losses on both sides. With a little
more pressure, the Southerners
might have broken; but there was no
extra pressure, and the
line held. Not until mid-afternoon
did the southern end of the Union
line attack. Across Antietam Bridge
(right) they stormed. Earlier
in the day, it would have made all
the difference. So late, it was simply a gallant charge instead of the
making of a decisive victory.
Still, Lee had to fall back across
the Potomac, the victory he so badly
needed still far out of reach.*

The fallen lay around Antietam Bridge, in Bloody Lane and in the fields near the Dunker Church (above). In all, the North lost 12,000 men, the South 11,000. Not only Lee had needed this battle; Lincoln too had been waiting for a victory and Antietam seemed to be near enough to the real thing. It was his intention

to give some meaning to this
slaughter and he had wanted the victory so that the deed would not
seem an act of weakness. Now, to
give the North and the world a sym-
bol of what the war was about, he
sat down and wrote the first
draft of the Emancipation Proclamation
which would set the Negro free:

I, Abraham Lincoln . . . hereby proclaim
that it is my purpose, upon the next meet-
ing of Congress to again recommend
the adoption of a practical measure tendering pecuniary aid to the free acceptance
or rejection of all slave-states so-called,
the people whereof may not then be in
rebellion against the United States,
and which States may then have voluntarily
adopted, or thereafter may voluntarily
adopt, immediate, or gradual abolishment
of slavery within their respective limits.

. . . that on the first day of January in the year of
our Lord, one thousand eight hundred
and sixty-three, all persons held as
slaves within any state, or designated part
of a state, the people whereof shall then
be in rebellion against the United
States, shall be then, thenceforward
and forever free . . .

*The note about the horses may very
well have been a reference to Jeb Stuart (left), the plumed knight of
the Confederacy, whose cavalry rode
around the Union men, be-deviled
their supply trains and fought bril-
liantly to delay the Union advance on
Antietam until Jackson and his men
could get back into the battle line.
Later on, Lincoln said flatly:*

Stuart's cavalry outmarched ours, having
certainly done more marked service
on the Peninsula, and everywhere since.

And so the Army of the Potomac got a new commander—General Ambrose Burnside (left)—and the army which had not been lucky in its leaders now had the worst. It was Burnside's notion that he could run quickly down the Rappahannock River, jump across before Lee knew he was there, and charge towards Richmond. Not surprisingly, when Burnside got on the river in December, Lee was opposite him and busily entrenching on Marye's Heights behind the town of Fredericksburg. There was no bridge over the river, but Burnside expected to build one— while Lee presumably just sat quietly.

Lincoln talked to Burnside about Fredericksburg (below) and then wired to General Henry "Old Brains" Halleck:

I have just had a long conference with Gen. Burnside. He believes that Gen. Lee's whole army, or nearly the whole of it is in front of him, at and near Fredericksburg. Gen. B. says he could take into

battle now any day, about, one hundred
and ten thousand men, that his army is in
good spirit, good condition, good
morale, and that in all respects he is
satisfied with officers and men; that he
does not want more men with him, because
he could not handle them to advantage,
that he thinks he can cross the
river in the face of the enemy and drive
him away, but that, to use his
own expression, it is somewhat risky.

Incredibly, Burnside tried to do it.
With his artillery (above) pounding
the town and ridge behind to
neutralize Confederate fire, a bridge
was pushed across the river. The
men in blue went over, through Fredericksburg and then started up
Marye's Heights. The slaughter was
terrible. In a few hours, the Army of
the Potomac had lost 13,000 men and
was back on its own side of the
river. It had never had a chance.

Lincoln saw the casualty lists (right) and wrote a "Congratulations To The Army of the Potomac" which must have struck the men in the ranks as ironic—or even worse:

I have just read your Commanding General's preliminary report of the battle of Fredericksburg. Although you were not successful, the attempt was not an error, nor the failure other than an accident. The courage with which you, in an open field, maintained the contest against an entrenched foe, and the consummate skill and success with which you crossed and recrossed the river, in the face of the enemy, show that you possess all the qualities of a great army, which will yet give victory to the cause of the country and of popular government. Condoling with the mourners of the dead, and sympathizing with the severely wounded, I congratulate you that the number of both is comparatively so small.

Again, the Union news was better from the west than the east. Farragut had one end of the Mississippi bottled up at New Orleans. Now, from the other end of the river, gun boats (above) were poking their way downstream. They were strange little craft with very shallow draft to get over the river sand bars, and with armour so light that most of the men who sailed them called them "tinclads." First, the Carondelet

dashed past the Confederate's for-
tified Island Number Ten and then
pecked away at the batteries below
to give the Union the river down to
the Tennessee border. Then the South
put together a fleet to fight at
Memphis, Tennessee, and the gunboats
and some rams whipped it. Now the
river was Union to the Mississippi
state line, and the Confederacy was in
danger of being cut right in two.

18

The Army of the Potomac spent a miserable winter (right) camped on the Rappahannock. From time to time, Burnside took them for a march in the mud, still hoping to surprise Lee. Neither the troops nor the President thought much of the maneuver. Lincoln wrote Halleck for advice:

Gen. Burnside wishes to cross the Rappahannock with his army, but his Grand Divisions Commanders oppose the movement. If in such a difficulty as this you do not help, you fail me precisely in the point for which I sought your assistance . . . gather all the elements for forming a judgement of your own; and then tell Gen. Burnside that you do approve, or that you do not approve his plan. Your military skill is useless to me, if you will not do this.

*The army had clearly lost faith in
Burnside; there had to be a new chief.
This time it was Fighting Joe
Hooker (right) and as spring came,
he had a plan. The Union cavalry was
to go west of Chancellorsville to
worry the Confederates. Then one
Union corps would cross the river
again at Fredericksburg to draw Lee
that way. Once he was drawn, the rest
of the Union army would leap over
the river near Chancellorsville, fall
upon the surprised Lee and destroy
him. Lee did go toward Fredericksburg
and Hooker did surprise him, but so
slowly that Lee was able to get his
men turned around and into line.
Then Lee pulled Jackson out of the
fight and sent him on an all day
march through the woods, all the
way around to the Union's open
right flank. Late that afternoon Jackson fe
upon the astonished Yankees and
Hooker was close to losing his whole
army when darkness intervened.
Through the third day, he clung
desperately to the river bank, then
Lee turned from him to deal with*

the Yankees attacking at Fredericksburg. It was a Confederate victory—but there had been a loss, a great one. Stonewall Jackson was dead, mortally wounded by a stray shot from one of his own men.

There were prisoners from these battles and those who flowed north lived about as well as prisoners ever do live in a war. The men taken south, though, went to an experience almost worse than battle itself.

The South had no desire to treat them badly, but food was scarce, there was hardly enough for the army. Men who lived through Andersonville, Georgia (below), were living skeletons when freed at the end of the war.

*Facilities for treating the wounded
were primitive and women of
both sides followed the armies
to help as only women could. The
most famous of them was a New
Englander, Clara Barton (right), who
served through the war and founded
the American Red Cross. Senator
Charles Sumner said of her, "She
has the talent of a statesman,
the command of a general
and the heart and hand of a woman."*

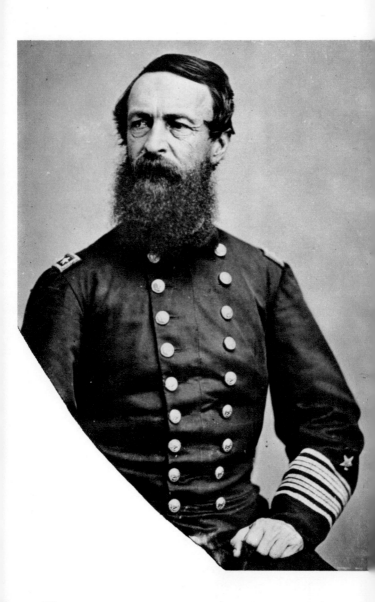

*The last Confederate stronghold on
the Mississippi was Vicksburg and
U. S. Grant had been harrying it, getting angrier and angrier with the
frustrating swamps that lay north of
the city. Now he marched his men
down the west bank of the river until they were south of the city and
Admiral David Porter (left), who had
handled Farragut's mortar boats
at New Orleans, ran his gunboats
past the blasting of Vicksburg's
batteries to join him. What was Gran
up to? He proposed to ferry his
men to the Vicksburg side of the
river, forget about his supply
lines and attack the city from the
south. The men could live off
the country. Over the river they
went and stodgier men said that this
time Grant had certainly ruined
his career. Instead, Grant ruined a
relief force heading for Vicksburg,
then settled down to a strangling
siege of the city. Lincoln noted:*

**Whether Gen. Grant shall or shall not
consummate the capture of Vicksburg, his
campaign from the beginning of this month
up to the twenty second day of it, is
one of the most brilliant in the world.**

*Then, in July, Vicksburg (above)
fell, starved out, and Lincoln wrote
Grant at length for the first time:*

I do not remember that you and I ever
met personally. I write this now as a
grateful acknowledgement for the almost
inestimable service you have done the
country. I wish to say a word further.
When you first reached the vicinity of
Vicksburg, I thought you should do, what

you finally did—march the troops across
the neck, run the batteries with the
transports and thus go below and I never
had any faith . . . that the Yazoo Pass
expedition and the like would succeed.
When you got below and took Port Gibson,
Grand Gulf and vicinity, I thought
you should go down the river and join
Gen. Banks; and when you turned
Northward East of the Big Black, I
feared it was a mistake. I now
wish to make the personal acknowledgement
that you were right, and I was wrong.

Back east, the South still needed
the big win and Lee headed for Pennsylvania again. Pleasant farm country
and sleepy farm towns like Gettysburg (above) lay in his path. Lincoln
wired Hooker to be off after him:

So far as we can make out here, the enemy
has Milroy surrounded at Winchester and
Tyler at Martinsburg . . . If the head
of Lee's army is at Martinsburg and the
tail of it on the Plank road between
Fredericksburg and Chancellorsville, the animal must be very
slim somewhere. Could you not break him?

*Hooker trailed Lee north, staying
between him and Washington; but with
the enemy clearly into Pennsylvania,
Lincoln decided that the loser at
Chancellorsville was not the man for
the next big fight. The new commander,
who had had a corps, was intelligent,
short tempered George Gordon Meade
(right). To supplement his efforts,
a Presidential Proclamation went out
calling for 100,000 militia to
rise and defend their homeland:*

**Whereas the armed insurrectionary com-
binations now existing in several of
the States are threatening to make inroads
into the states of Maryland, Western
Virginia, Pennsylvania and Ohio, requir-
ing immediately an additional military
force for the service of the United States.**

*Lee's men (left) tramped north and
they believed they could whip any
army in the world. Through southern
Pennsylvania they raided, taking the
shoes and food they needed so badly.
Then Lee pulled his groups southeast,
concentrating to face the Army
of the Potomac which they had defeat-
ed so often before. Meade, the new
commander, was putting out cavalry,
feeling for his foe. He had a notion
that he wanted to make his stand
along Pipe Creek, but two great
armies were coming together—75,000
Southerners, 87,000 Northerners—
and where they collided was the
place the fight was going to be.
Back in Washington, Lincoln
had been feeling a little more com-
fortable and telling Mrs. Lincoln:*

**I do not think the raid into Pennsylvania
amounts to anything at all.**

On June 30, General John Buford
(right) and his division of cavalry
came clattering into Gettysburg;
to Buford, this town looked like
the place where Lee's men would
come together. Heavy patrols went out
the roads running west and north,
and Buford figured he was in for a
fight in the morning. Morning
proved him right. In from the west,
came a Confederate corps—A. P.
Hill's—and the Union cavalrymen
fought, dismounted, from a ridge just
west of the town. For two hours
they held, then Reynolds' corps
came up for the Union to jar the
Confederate advance back on its
heels. It was the last good Northern
moment of the day. A sharpshooter
got Reynolds and Ewell brought
another Confederate corps onto the
field from the north. Union troops
came all through the day, but
there weren't enough of them and by
nightfall they were scrambling
back through the town, forming a
shaky line on Cemetery Hill which
Ewell might have knocked to pieces,
had he put more into a last, hard thrust.

Through a wild night, Meade got the
rest of his men onto the battlefield.
His right lay on Culp's Hill which
faced north, his center and left on
Cemetery hill which curved down
from Culp's to face west. On the second day Lee planned to hit the left
with General James Longstreet's corps,
and the right with peg-legged Richard
Ewell's corps. Co-ordination went
sour and the attacks did not go well,
but Longstreet's men did cut up Union
politician-general Dan Sickles' corps
which the eccentric Sickles had post-
ed further forward than Meade had
ordered. The bullets flew so thickly
that day that the very trees
were pock-marked with them (right).

The nearest thing to a real Confederate success that day came when fire-eating General John Hood saw a hill on the south of the Union line—Little Round Top—unoccupied and sent his men swarming up it. If he could have held the hill, he could have rolled up the whole Yankee line, but Union General Gouverneur Warren organized a counter-attack. There was a hand-to-hand brawl at the top of the hill and then the Confederates were back across the way, sniping from Devil's Den (right).

The next day was July 3, 1863 and it
is probably the most famous single
day in American military history.
Having pounded the Union wings, Lee
decided that a smash at their center
would go through to victory. To
do the job there were 15,000 men
under the command of General George
Pickett (right). Legend has it
that they were Virginians, but ac-
tually there were men from almost
all the Confederate states present.
At one in the afternoon, the Confederate artillery opened, seeking
to pound down the Union guns which
had beaten them at Malvern Hill. The
bombardment and the counter-battery
went on for an hour, then the Union
guns went silent. Pickett sent his
men out and before them lay a
wide, shallow valley which rose to
a low ridge where the Yankees lay.
The Union artillery went at it again;
they had shut down only to save
ammunition, and big holes began to
appear in the beautifully even
ranks. But the Confederates marched

*until they were close enough for
the Union infantrymen to join
in the fire. Then a great rebel yell
rose from Pickett's men and they
went forward at the double into the
Union line. Here and there, a
few of them broke through, but there
were too many guns and too many
tough Yankees with bayonets. Back
they went and Lee said, "It is all my
fault." No matter whose fault it was,
the Confederate States of America had
come as far north as they were to go.*

*On the Fourth of July, Lin-
coln told the country the news:*

**The President announces to the country
that news from the Army of the Potomac . . .
is such as to cover that Army with the**

highest honor, to promise a great
success to the cause of the Union, and
to claim the condolence of all for
the many gallant fallen. And that for
this, he especially desires on this day,
He whose will, not ours, should ever
be done, be everywhere remembered and
reverenced with profoundest gratitude.

*The decisive victory, the smashing of
the Army of Northern Virginia for
which Lincoln had hoped, was not to be.
Lee made his way back south and
Meade was not the man to follow him
hard enough to get in a death blow.
Still, the South faced the
future knowing that it had missed*

the big victory, the victory it
had to have to win English support,
knowing that it was cut in two
along the line of the Mississippi,
knowing that every day the
blockade was getting tighter. There
would be two more years of war, but
night was settling on the Confederacy.

The casualties were enormous. Lee had some 28,000 killed and wounded, Meade 23,000. For the Union men, there were at least the crude hospitals (below) near the field. One who survived them said later, "It was dark and the building lighted partially with candles. All around . . . lay the wounded men, some cursing and swearing and some praying; in the middle of the room there was some 10 or 12 tables with just

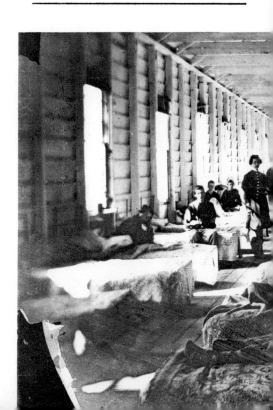

*enough to lay a man on; these were
used as dissecting tables and
they were covered with blood . . . By
the side of the tables was a heap
of feet, legs and arms. On one
of these I was laid and . . . (the
surgeon) felt in my mouth and then
wanted to give me chloroform; this
I refused to take and he took a pair
of scissors and cut out the pieces
of bone in my mouth; then gave me a
drink of whiskey and had me laid away."*

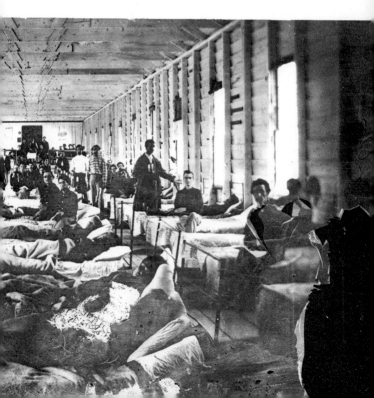

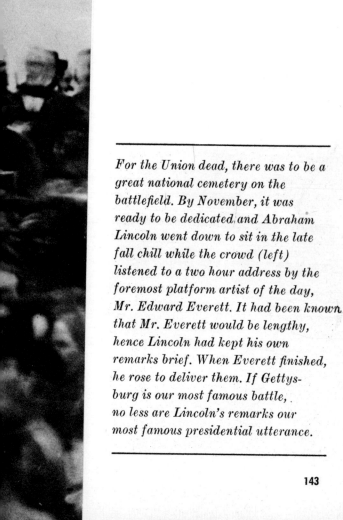

For the Union dead, there was to be a great national cemetery on the battlefield. By November, it was ready to be dedicated and Abraham Lincoln went down to sit in the late fall chill while the crowd (left) listened to a two hour address by the foremost platform artist of the day, Mr. Edward Everett. It had been known that Mr. Everett would be lengthy, hence Lincoln had kept his own remarks brief. When Everett finished, he rose to deliver them. If Gettysburg is our most famous battle, no less are Lincoln's remarks our most famous presidential utterance.

Four score and seven years ago, our
fathers brought forth on this continent, a
new nation, conceived in Liberty and
dedicated to the proposition
that all men are created equal.

Now we are engaged in a great civil war,
testing whether that nation or
any nation so conceived and so dedicated,
can long endure. We are met on a great
battlefield of that war. We have come
to dedicate a portion of that field,
as a final resting place for those
who here gave their lives that that
nation might live. It is altogether fit-
ting and proper that we should do this.

But, in a larger sense, we can not
dedicate—we can not consecrate—we can
not hallow—this ground. The brave men,
living and dead, who struggled here,

have consecrated it, far above our poor
power to add or detract. The world will
little note, nor long remember, what
we say here, but it can never forget
what they did here. It is for us
the living, rather, to be dedicated here
to the unfinished work which they who
fought here have thus far so nobly
advanced. It is rather for us to be
here dedicated to the great task remain-
ing before us—that from these honored
dead we take increased devotion to
that cause for which they gave the last
full measure of devotion—that we
here highly resolve that these dead shall
not have died in vain—that this
nation, under God, shall have a new
birth of freedom—and that government
of the people, by the people, for the
people, shall not perish from the earth.

*In eastern Tennessee that summer, a
Union army under General William
Rosecrans was nosing dangerously
close to Georgia and Alabama.
Part of Longstreet's corps
went out to help send Rosecrans
reeling back north.
The armies met along Chickamauga Creek in September. All
one day the armies battered each other.
Then on the second day an order
was misread, a Union division pulled
out of the center of the line, and
Longstreet's men went whooping
through the hole to send most of the
Yankees streaming back toward
Chattanooga. Only General George
Thomas (right) stood firm. On a
little ridge, he drew up what was
left of his own corps and any strag-
glers he could lay hands on.
In the end, Bragg had
the field, but at the cost of so
many casualties that he could
not strike another blow. To the north
Thomas was "The Rock of Chickamauga"
and Lincoln wrote a friend:*

It is doubtful whether his heroism
and skill exhibited last Sunday afternoon,
was ever surpassed in the world.

*Still, Bragg had his enemy bottled up
in Chattanooga which he could
watch from the commanding Missionary
Ridge (below). U. S. Grant was sent
along to alleviate the situation.
It was no small task; Grant
fancied no one could get straight up
the ridge, but perhaps General
William T. Sherman could get around
it on the north while Fighting Joe
Hooker harassed it on the south. In
the center, Thomas and his men
were to demonstrate just enough to
keep the Confederates busy. Sherman
ran into hard going. Hooker—to*

*everyone's surprise—climbed all
the way up Lookout Mountain, but
the ridge still held. Grant ordered
Thomas's men forward to the foot
of the ridge—just a little diversion
to take pressure off Sherman.
Forward they went and while Grant
and Thomas gaped, kept right
on going up the ridge and over it,
while the Confederates fled. A delighted
Lincoln wrote Grant:*

**Your despatches as to fight on
Monday and Tuesday are here. Well done.
Many thanks to all.**

18

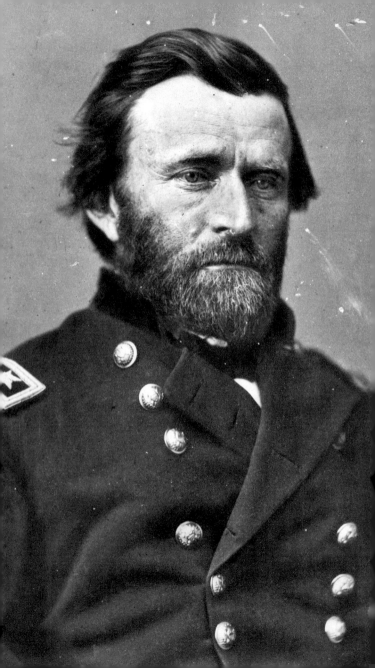

Lincoln made up his mind.
Meade would remain in command of the
Army of the Potomac, but U. S. Grant (left)
would be brought east to be supreme
commander of all the Northern armies.
In a speech when Grant arrived in
Washington, the President said:

The nation's appreciation of what you have
done and its reliance upon you for what
remains to do, in the existing great
struggle, are now presented with this com-
mission, constituting you Lieutenant General in the Army of the United States.
With this high honor devolves upon
you also, a corresponding responsibility.
As the country herein trusts you, so,
under God, it will sustain you.
I scarcely need to add that with what
I here speak for the nation
goes my own hearty personal concurrence.

And the next day there was a note to Grant:

Mrs. L invites yourself and General
Meade to dine with us Saturday evening.
Please notify him, and answer
whether you can be with us at that time.

While the armies camped and
waited for spring and dry roads,
Grant made his plans. He would attack
straight toward Richmond. Lee must
come out to fight him and once
the fight started Grant would keep
it up day after day, week after week
in a war of attrition the North
could afford far better than the
South. From the west, Sherman, now
in command, would drive for Atlanta,
destroying food, factories,
everything the South had which could
help them keep on fighting the war.
Then the men and the wagons headed
south and Lincoln wrote Grant:

Not expecting to see you again before the
Spring campaign begins, I wish to
express in this way, my entire
satisfaction with what you have done
up to this time, so far as I understand
it. The particulars of your plans
I neither know, or seek to know. You
are vigilant and self reliant; and pleased
with this, I wish not to obtrude any
constraints or restraints upon
you. While I am very anxious that
any great disaster, or the capture
of our men in great numbers, shall be
avoided, I know these points are less
likely to escape your attention than
they would be mine. If there is anything
wanting which it is within my power to
give, do not fail to let me know it.

And now with a brave Army
and a just cause, may God sustain you.

Grant was moving along narrow, winding roads into the Wilderness (left), a vast tangle of second growth scrub and trees in northern Virginia. Lee let him get into the thickets and then struck. For two days, the armies ravaged one another in undergrowth so thick that a man was hard put to see more than a few feet. The brush caught fire and wounded burned to death. By the end of the second day, Grant had an appalling 17,000 casualties. When Lee heard men and wagons moving in the night, he assumed, not unreasonably, that Grant had made his fight, failed to break the Army of Northern Virginia and was heading home to lick his wounds. Not Grant, though— he was simply sliding to the left, going around Lee's flank and deeper still into Virginia. At a band concert, Lincoln said:

Ladies and gentlemen, you, no doubt desire to have a speech from me. In lieu of a speech, I propose that we give three cheers for General Grant and all the armies under his command.

157

The new battleground was
Spottsylvania and for two more days
there was an awful slaughter,
more work than the burial parties
(right) could handle. The North
could replace its losses, the South
could not. Grant slid left again
to go further south and in
spite of the casualty lists, Lin-
coln supported him to the hilt:

I think, without knowing the particulars
of the plans of General Grant, that
what has been accomplished is of
more importance than at first appears.
I believe I know that Gen. Grant has
not been jostled from his purpose.

Grant (below, seated by tree, head down) stood before Cold Harbor, miscalculated and put in an attack that cost 5,000 men in ten minutes. It was a jolt, but he went on south, aiming to get to the James River, across it and in on Petersburg, the vital railroad center south of Richmond.

Grim William T. Sherman (right)
also started to move south in early
May and just before he departed
Chattanooga, Lincoln wrote him:

I have an imploring appeal in behalf of
the Citizens who say your order No. 8 will
compel them to go North ... This is, in no
sense, an order; nor is it even
a request that you will do anything
which, in the least, shall be a drawback
upon your military operations, but
any thing you can do consistently
with those operations, for these suf-
fering people, I shall be glad of.

Sherman snapped back, "It is
demonstrated that the railroad can-
not support the army and the people
too. One or the other must
quit and the army don't intend
to unless Joe Johnston makes us."

Joe Johnston (right) couldn't make Sherman do anything. The Yankees had a slight edge in manpower, but their general preferred to slip around Johnston's flanks, leaving him a choice of falling back or being encircled. Johnston fell back, saving his men, waiting for an enemy mistake. In Richmond, Jefferson Davis, who never cared for Johnston anyway, was becoming impatient. When Sherman slipped over the Chattahoochee River, the last good defense line outside Atlanta, Georgia, Davis could stand no more. Out went Johnston and in came John Hood who, if he could do nothing else, could attack like the devil himself. Sherman braced to receive him.

If Grant got across the James River, he would eventually break the railroad lines and Petersburg and Richmond would fall. It is no great thing to cross a river, but Grant had to do it without being observed by Lee. If Lee caught him with half his army on one side, half on the other, the Army of the Potomac was likely to go under in the process. Accordingly, the Union cavalry feinted north of Richmond and before Lee saw through it, Grant had his pontoons (right) over the James and his army across. Meanwhile, Lincoln had been re-nominated for the presidency and to some visiting well wishers, said:

I suppose that you have done me this kindness in connection with the action of the Baltimore convention which has recently taken place, and with which of course, I am very well satisfied (laughter). What we want, still more than Baltimore conventions or presidential elections is, success under Gen. Grant.

B-159

If you had been Robert E. Lee in the
summer of 1864, you might well have
asked, "What am I to do?" The key
to Richmond was threatened. If the
city went, the rickety Confederate
government would go with it. Lee
had too few men to attack; he waited.

*Lincoln saw the climax at hand and
wired Grant when he had crossed the James
River and set up his new base (above):*

**Have just read your despatch of
1 PM yesterday. I begin to see it. You
will succeed. God bless you all.**

At sea, there was more good news for the President. The Confederate commerce raider *Alabama*, commanded by Captain Raphael Semmes, had been a devil on the seas, making a hash of Union shipping. Now, the U.S.S. *Kearsarge*, Captain John Winslow, (*center, below*) commanding, had caught her coming out of Cherbourg, France and sent her down in a stand-up ship to ship fight.

Lincoln sent Congress word:

I most cordially recommend that Captain
John A. Winslow, U.S. Navy, receive
a vote of Thanks from Congress, for the
skill and gallantry exhibited by him
in the brilliant action, whilst in
command of the U.S.S. Steamer Kearsarge
which led to the total destruction of the Piratical craft Alabama
on the 19 June, 1864—a vessel
superior in tonnage, superior in number
of guns and superior in number of crew.

*And there was more good news at sea.
There were two holes left in the
blockade by which blockade runners
could slip in to carry goods to the
faltering Confederacy. One was at
Fort Fisher, North Carolina, the other at
Mobile Bay, Alabama. For Mobile Bay,
old salt Farragut was called in
once again. Against him was a channel
full of mines (torpedoes, they
called them in those days) and the
usual forts. Farragut went in, his
gunners (left) at battle stations.
The monitor* Tecumsah *hit a torpedo
and sank; Farragut yelled "Damn
the torpedoes! Full speed ahead!"
They sailed past the forts. The Rebel*
Tennessee *came out and a monitor
hammered her into surrender. The Confederacy had exactly one port left.
Lincoln wrote to his prized old salt:*

The national thanks are tendered by the
President to Admiral Farragut and
Major General Canby for the skill and
harmony with which the recent
operations into Mobile Harbor . . . were
planned and carried into execution.

*Uncle Billy Sherman's boys (above)
were in front of Atlanta and nothing
was surer than that John Hood would
be coming out to fight them. The
Texan tried to get around Sherman's
flank north of the city; he gained
nothing and lost men. Still,
Sherman couldn't get in; the lines
were too strong. Uncle Billy
left a screen and moved the bulk of
his force south to cut off Hood's*

railroad. *Hood pulled out and Sher-*
man sent Lincoln: "Atlanta is ours and
fairly won." Lincoln sent him back:

The national thanks are herewith tendered
by the President to Major General
William T. Sherman and the gallant officers and soldiers of his command before
Atlanta, for the distinguished ability,
courage and perseverance displayed in
the campaign in Georgia which . . . has result-
ed in the capture of the city of Atlanta.

175

Atlanta (below) was his. Sherman was now free to repeat Grant's gambit: to cut loose from his supply line and march to the sea. He set out to "make Georgia howl." There was nothing much in front of him; he was able to send the President Savannah for a Christ-

When you were about leaving Atlanta for the Atlantic coast, I was anxious, if not fearful, but feeling that you were the better judge, and remembering that ''nothing risked, nothing gained'' I did not interfere. Now the undertaking being a success, the honor is all yours.

*It had been easier to get in front of
Petersburg than take the place.
Grant was there, but the stubborn,
weary and hungry Confederates held on
inside their fortifications. He settled down to siege (right) and once
more, Lincoln backed him all the way:*

I have seen your despatch expressing
your unwillingness to break your
hold where you are. Neither am I willing. Hold on with a bull-dog grip,
and chew & choke, as much as possible.

*To break the ring around Petersburg,
there was a scheme for a regiment
of Pennsylvania miners to dig a tunnel into the line, fill it
with gun powder and blow the whole
thing to blazes. They dug, the powder was laid and the mine went up.
The result was a wasteland like the
surface of the moon (right); but
the follow-up assault was under none
other than Burnside of Fredericksburg fame, and the result was a
bungled affair which went so slowly
that the shaken Confederates
were able to get themselves reorganized and toss the stormers out
of their lines with heavy casualties.*

Lee had one more wriggle left: the old trick from McClellan's Peninsula campaign—to threaten Washington with a force in the Shenandoah Valley. Jackson was gone; General Jubal Early was sent to do the job and he gave Lincoln a bad case of trembles. He sent Grant a most urgent message:

Now what I think is that you should provide to retain your hold where you are certainly, and bring the rest with you personally, and make a vigorous effort to destroy the enemy's force in this vicinity. I think there is really a fair chance to do this if the movement if prompt. This is what I think, upon your suggestion, and it is not an order.

Very well—no order. Instead of coming himself, Grant sent General Phil Sheridan (left, seated center). Lincoln seemed well pleased:

I have seen your despatch in which you say ''I want Sheridan put in command of all the troops in the field, with instructions to put himself South of the enemy and follow him to the death. Wherever the enemy goes, let our troops go also.'' This, I think, is exactly right.

*In September, Sheridan came up
against Early at Winchester, Virginia,
and while his infantry pinned the
Confederate line, his cavalry—with
wild young horsemen like George Custer
(left) who would die later at Little
Big Horn—swept around the flank
and sent the Southerners running as
no Yankee had ever seen them run
before. Near Fisher's Hill, Early
stood and again Sheridan flanked him
out of the position. Lincoln wired:*

**Have just heard of your great victory. God
bless you all, officers and men.
Strongly inclined to come and see you.**

---

*Early made one more attack. It went
well at first, but Sheridan came gal-
loping up from twenty miles back of
the line to rally his men and win.
The Shenandoah was now out of the war.*

*The elections were coming on, Peters-
burg still held out and Lincoln
(right) had serious doubts as to
whether a war weary nation would re-
elect him. He wrote himself a memo:*

**This morning, as for some days past, it
seems exceedingly probable that this
Administration will not be re-elected.
Then it will be my duty to so co-operate
with the President-elect, as to
save the Union between the election and
the inauguration; as he will have se-
cured his election on such ground that
he cannot possibly save it afterwards.**

---

*The President could have saved his
worry. Grant might be stalled, but
the victories of Sherman and Sheridan
swept him back for a second term.*

Grant held Lee at Petersburg, Sher-
man harried a pitiful little force
now back under Joe Johnston in
the South. There was still one more
Confederate outfit, though, the army
John Hood (left) had led from Atlanta.
This impetuous Texan was now push-
ing up towards Nashville, Tennes-
see. There stood Thomas, "The Rock
of Chickamauga." "Old Slow Trot" they
called him in the service—and he
drove both Grant and Lincoln nearly
to fits by not attacking until he
was absolutely ready. When he did at-
tack over cold December fields, it
was a two day battle, then a rout
with Confederates flying south,
no longer an army. Thomas followed
the pursuit and his cavalry com-
mander James Wilson heard him calling
out of the dark, "Dang it to hell,
Wilson, didn't I tell you we could
lick 'em, didn't I tell you we could
lick 'em?" Lincoln congratulated him:

Please accept for yourselves, officers
and men, the nation's thanks for your
good work of yesterday. You made a magnificent beginning. A grand consummation is
within your easy reach. Do not let it slip.

18

65

For the shrinking South, there was
still one window on the world—Fort
Fisher at Wilmington, North Carolina.
Porter took the largest fleet the
United States had ever assembled
(above) to bombard it, then sent
infantry ashore.
A happy Lincoln said:

Sir: It is my agreeable duty to enclose
herewith a joint resolution approved 24th
January, 1865, tendering the thanks
of Congress to yourself, the officers
and men under your command, for their gallantry and good conduct in the capture
of Fort Fisher, and through you to all
who participated in that brilliant
and decisive victory under your command.

It was March and the war was clearly drawing to an end. As Lincoln stood before the Capitol (left) to deliver his Inaugural Address, he tried to face the nation toward the task of making peace which lay ahead:

... with malice toward none; with charity for all; with firmness in the right, as God gives us to see the right, let us strive on to finish the work we are in; to bind up the nation's wounds; to care for him who shall have borne the battle, and for his widow and his orphan —to do all which may achieve and cherish a just and a lasting peace, among ourselves, and with all nations.

195

Lee's men in the Petersburg lines were so few and so hungry. Grant extended a flank and they had to extend to cover him—then suddenly, they were extended too far and the Union men were pouring through all along the line. Petersburg fell, then Richmond (below), flaming in an accidental fire. Lincoln wrote Grant:

Gen. Sheridan says ''If the thing is pressed I think that Lee will surrender.'' Let the thing be pressed.

The thing was pressed. Hard marching Yankees raced along Lee's flank to get across his line of retreat. It could be only hours before there was no more war, no more dead boys, no more letters from Lincoln to heart-broken women like Mrs. Bixby:

Dear Madame—I have just been shown in the files of the War Department a statement of the Adjutant General of Massachusetts, that you are the mother of five sons who have died gloriously on the field of battle. I feel how weak and fruitless must be any words of mine which should attempt to beguile you from the grief of a loss so overwhelming. But I cannot refrain from tendering to you the consolation that may be found in the thanks of the Republic they died to save.

I pray that our Heavenly Father may assuage the anguish of your bereavement and leave you only the cherished memory of the loved and lost, and the solemn pride that must be yours, to have laid so costly a sacrifice upon the altar of Freedom.

Lee's men trudged west and at Appo-
mattox Court House they found Union
troops ahead of them. The govern-
ment of the Confederacy was in flight;
the last army was starving and in
rags. They had done all men could do
and Lee did the only thing left to do.
He and Grant met in the home of a
Mr. McClean (below) and the war was
over. Lincoln sent a message to the
War Department for his son, Tad:

Tad wants some flags. Can he be accommodated?

We meet this evening, not in sorrow, but
in gladness of heart. The evacuation
of Petersburg and Richmond and the surrender of the principal insurgent army
give hope of a righteous and speedy peace.

*This was Abraham Lincoln's last
public utterance. A half-mad actor,
John Wilkes Booth, shot him as he sat
in Ford's Theater. He was carried
to a home across the street from the
theater to die—and with him died
the South's best chance of a fruitful
peace. The avengers would take
over the task now that he was gone.*

The army shot Booth (left) as he hid
in a barn. Four more of the con-
spirators (left, from the top)—Mary
Surratt, Lewis Payne, George Atze-
rodt and David Herald—were hung
(above) at Washington Penitentiary.

*The poet Walt Whitman gave words
to the nation's grief as a funeral
train (right) carried Lincoln
to rest at Springfield, Illinois:*

•

*Coffin that passes through lanes and
streets,
Through day and night with the great
cloud darkening the land,
With the pomp of the inloop'd flags
with the cities draped in black,
With the show of the States themselves as of crape-veil'd
women standing,
With processions long and winding and
the flambeaus of the night,
With the countless torches lit, with
the silent seas of faces and the
unbared heads,
With the waiting depot, the arriving
coffin and the sombre faces,
With dirges through the night, with
the thousand voices rising strong
and solemn,
With all the mournful voices of the
dirges pour'd around the coffin,
The dim-lit churches and the shudder-
ing organs—where amid these
you journey,
With the tolling tolling bell's perpetual clang,
Here, coffin that slowly passes,
I give you my sprig of lilac.*

The Southerners went home and Grant had let those who had horses keep them to help get in a spring crop. The victorious Northerners paraded in Washington (right)—the eastern men whom the Confederates had once despised as "clerks" and the western farmers who had marched with Sherman. It was all over now; the Union was one and a man who was there when Lee surrendered wrote, ". . . it was felt by all that peace had at last dawned upon the land. The charges were now withdrawn from the guns, the campfires were left to smoulder in their ashes, the flags were tenderly furled . . . and the Army of the Union and the Army of Northern Virginia turned their backs upon each other for the first time in four long, bloody years."
A private had summed it up earlier for the soldiers: "Death is the common lot of all and the difference between dying to day and to morrow is not much, but we all prefer to morrow."

ABOUT THE PHOTOGRAPHER

Most of the photographs in this book were made by Mathew Brady (right) or by photographers working for him. Born in upstate New York about 1823, Brady came to the city as a young man and first learned photography from lectures given by Samuel F. B. Morse, the famous inventor. Morse had seen Daguerreotypes made in France. Brady was only 21 when he opened his own studio at Broadway and Fulton Street. Ingeniously experimenting with skylights in the roof and with reflectors, the young man became the city's leading portrait photographer. Even so early, his journalist's instinct led him to attempt to make a complete photographic record of all the notables of his day. To this end, he opened a second gallery in Washington.

When the war came, it seemed to release some deep instinct in the man. He said later, "I felt that I had to go—and I went." Neglecting his studio practice, he took the field with

211

the troops and when the task became too great for one man, hired assistants to cover areas he could not reach personally. Two of his assistants, Alexander Gardner and Timothy O'Sullivan, became famous in their own right.

The work involved in their pictures was remarkably complicated. The most advanced process was the wet collodion plate. A chemical mixture was first poured on a glass plate. The plate was then sensitized in a mixture of water and silver nitrate and placed in the camera still wet. The exposure was then made and the plate rushed immediately to the wagon dark room (right) for developing. Plates were often as large as a shirt cardboard.

An active collaborator in the venture was Edward Anthony, the photographic supply dealer whose firm eventually became the Ansco Company. Anthony allowed Brady large credits for equipment when his own resources proved unequal to the task. After the war, when Brady ran into serious financial difficulties, he sold one set of his negatives to Anthony. This set was eventually placed in the Library of Congress. A second set was purchased by the government and is now cared for in the National Archives. A final group of plates were found recently in Oswego, New York. Ansco—which kindly supplied many of the prints for this book—acquired these and now has them in the National Archives for safekeeping.

Brady was not the first war correspondent with a camera; Roger Fenton had earlier made pictures of the Crimean conflict. No one previously, however, had attempted to cover an entire war and certainly no single photographer has ever covered a war better. His portraits of the leaders and men are unsurpassed and many of his scenes could not be improved upon today by men working with the most modern equipment. No photographer has ever left a body of work of such magnificent quality and historical interest.

A NOTE ON THE PICTURES

The photographs in this book were all
reproduced from original glass-plate
negatives either by direct contact
printing or from copy negatives. In one
or two cases, where the original plates
were lost or destroyed, the reproduction
was made from an early printed copy
or a carte-de-visite sepia positive.
While some of the pictures have been
cropped for visual effect, as an aid to
design, every effort has been made to
preserve the flavor of these 100-year-old
negatives: water-damaged emulsions,
breaks, cracks or chips in the glass
negatives, tones faded by age, and
scratches or bruises in the too-frequently
handled plate surfaces have all been
preserved as they appear in the
negatives now stored carefully in
Washington.

PICTURE SOURCES

There are two great Brady Collections.
One is at the National Archives, the
other at the Library of Congress. Both
are in Washington, D. C. Anyone may
visit either collection and prints are
available for a nominal charge. Both
have microfilm records of their
Brady Collections which are available